A Journey Of Justice, Integrity, And Legacy Stephen Breyer

An Intimate Portrait of the Supreme Court Justice Who Shaped American Jurisprudence

Julia J. Scott

Copyright © 2024 Julia J. Scott

All rights reserved. No part of this publication may be reproduced, distributed, or transmitted in any form or by any means, including photocopying, recording, or other electronic or mechanical methods, without the prior written permission of the publisher, except in the case of brief quotations embodied in critical reviews and certain other noncommercial uses permitted by copyright law.

Table Of Contents

Introduction
Chapter One; Childhood and Education
Chapter Two; Early Career
Chapter Three; Judicial Appointment
Chapter Four; Supreme Court Tenure
Chapter Five; Legacy and Impact
Chapter Six; Personal Life
Chapter Seven; Retirement and Post-Court Activities
Conclusion

Introduction

In a world where the echoes of justice resound through the hallowed halls of the highest court in the land, one man stood as a beacon of integrity, intellect, and unwavering commitment to the rule of law.

His name: Stephen Breyer. Welcome to the captivating odyssey of a jurist whose journey from humble beginnings to the pinnacle of the legal profession is a testament to the power of perseverance, passion, and principled leadership.

Join me on a riveting exploration of the life and legacy of Stephen Breyer, a jurist whose impact reverberates far beyond the walls of the Supreme Court of the United States. From his formative years in San Francisco to his tenure on the highest court in the land, Breyer's story is one of courage, conviction, and the relentless pursuit of justice.

As we delve into the pages of this biography, prepare to be enthralled by the twists and turns of Breyer's remarkable journey. From his early days as a law clerk to his pivotal role in shaping American jurisprudence, Breyer's life is a testament to the enduring power of the law to shape the course of history and transform the lives of individuals and communities.

Through meticulous research, intimate interviews, and vivid storytelling, this biography seeks to illuminate the man behind the robe, offering readers a rare glimpse into the heart and mind of one of the most influential jurists of our time.

From his landmark opinions on the Court to his personal passions and pursuits, we will uncover the myriad facets of Breyer's character, values, and contributions to the legal profession and society as a whole.

But beyond the courtroom drama and legal intrigue, this biography also offers a deeply human portrait of a man who, despite the weight of his responsibilities, remains grounded in the values of family, friendship, and lifelong learning.

As we journey through the pages of Breyer's life, we will discover the personal experiences, passions, and principles that have shaped his journey and fueled his commitment to justice and equality under the law. So, dear reader, buckle up and prepare to embark on an unforgettable odyssey through the life and legacy of Stephen Breyer.

From the halls of justice to the corridors of power, join me as we uncover the untold stories, hidden truths, and enduring principles that define the remarkable journey of one of America's most distinguished jurists.

Chapter One; Childhood and Education

Stephen Breyer's early years were shaped by his upbringing in San Francisco, California. Born on August 15, 1938, he grew up in a close-knit family environment, surrounded by the bustling city life of San Francisco. From a young age, Breyer exhibited a keen intellect and a curiosity about the world around him.

Breyer's educational journey began at Lowell High School, a prestigious public school known for its academic rigor. During his time at Lowell, Breyer excelled academically, demonstrating a passion for learning and a knack for critical thinking.

He actively participated in extracurricular activities and developed a reputation as a dedicated and hardworking student. After graduating from Lowell High School, Breyer continued his academic pursuits at Stanford University.

At Stanford, he pursued a diverse range of interests, studying subjects such as philosophy, political science, and economics. Breyer's time at Stanford broadened his intellectual horizons and provided him with a solid foundation in liberal arts education.

Following his undergraduate studies, Breyer attended Magdalen College, Oxford, as a Marshall Scholar. At Oxford, he delved deeper into his academic interests, focusing on philosophy, politics, and economics.

The experience of studying abroad exposed Breyer to new ideas and perspectives, further shaping his intellectual development. Upon returning to the United States, Breyer enrolled at Harvard Law School, where he continued to distinguish himself as a bright and ambitious student.

He immersed himself in the study of law, captivated by the complexities of legal reasoning and jurisprudence. Breyer's time at Harvard Law School laid the groundwork for his future career in law and public service.

Throughout his educational journey, Breyer demonstrated a voracious appetite for knowledge and a commitment to academic excellence. His formative years instilled in him a deep appreciation for learning and a sense of intellectual curiosity that would define his lifelong pursuit of knowledge.

In addition to his academic pursuits, Breyer's childhood was also shaped by his family life and upbringing in San Francisco. He fondly recalls spending time with his parents and siblings, cherishing the moments spent exploring the city and engaging in family activities.

Breyer's upbringing instilled in him values of hard work, integrity, and compassion, which would guide him throughout his life and career. Overall, Stephen Breyer's childhood and education laid the foundation for his future success and achievements.

From his early years in San Francisco to his academic journey at prestigious institutions, Breyer's formative experiences shaped him into the accomplished scholar, jurist, and public servant that he would later become.

After completing his education, Stephen Breyer embarked on a remarkable journey that would lead him to become one of the most respected legal minds in the United States. Armed with his academic achievements and a passion for justice, Breyer set out to make a meaningful impact in the world of law and public service.

Breyer's early career saw him gain valuable experience in both academia and government. He served as a law clerk for Supreme Court Justice Arthur Goldberg, where he gained firsthand insight into the inner workings of the judicial system.

This experience provided Breyer with invaluable exposure to the complexities of constitutional law and the Supreme Court's role in shaping American jurisprudence. Following his clerkship, Breyer embarked on a career in academia, teaching at prestigious institutions such as Harvard Law School and the Kennedy School of Government.

As a scholar, Breyer delved into various areas of law, publishing influential works on topics ranging from administrative law to regulatory policy. His scholarly contributions earned him recognition as a leading authority in his field and laid the groundwork for his future endeavors.

In addition to his academic pursuits, Breyer also dedicated himself to public service, serving in various government roles throughout his career. He held positions in the Department of Justice and the Senate Judiciary Committee, where he played a key role in shaping legislation and policy on issues such as antitrust law and criminal justice reform.

Breyer's commitment to public service underscored his belief in the importance of civic engagement and the rule of law. In 1980, Breyer's career took a significant turn when he was appointed to the U.S. Court of Appeals for the First Circuit by President Jimmy Carter.

During his tenure on the First Circuit, Breyer distinguished himself as a fair and thoughtful jurist, earning praise for his reasoned opinions and commitment to upholding the rule of law. His experience on the appellate court prepared him for the next chapter of his career: a seat on the highest court in the land.

In 1994, President Bill Clinton nominated Stephen Breyer to serve as an Associate Justice of the Supreme Court of the United States. Confirmed by the Senate with overwhelming bipartisan support, Breyer took his place on the nation's highest court, where he would serve with distinction for nearly three decades.

Throughout his tenure on the Supreme Court, Breyer emerged as a pragmatic and thoughtful voice on the bench. He approached each case with careful consideration, weighing the legal arguments and implications before reaching his decision. Breyer's opinions reflected a deep respect for precedent and a commitment to interpreting the law in a manner consistent with its underlying principles.

In addition to his judicial responsibilities, Breyer also played an active role in the administration of the court, serving on various committees and task forces. He worked tirelessly to improve the efficiency and effectiveness of the judicial system, advocating for reforms to enhance access to justice and promote transparency in the legal process.

As he reflected on his tenure on the Supreme Court, Breyer expressed gratitude for the opportunity to serve his country and contribute to the administration of justice. He remained committed to upholding the rule of law and protecting the rights and freedoms enshrined in the Constitution, ensuring that the principles of justice and equality would endure for future generations.

In addition, Stephen Breyer's journey from his humble beginnings in San Francisco to his esteemed position on the Supreme Court is a testament to the power of education, hard work, and dedication.

His lifelong commitment to justice and public service has left an indelible mark on the legal profession and the nation as a whole, inspiring countless individuals to follow in his footsteps and uphold the values of fairness, integrity, and equality under the law.

Chapter Two; Early Career

Stephen Breyer's early career was characterized by a blend of academic scholarship, government service, and legal practice. After completing his education, Breyer embarked on a path that would ultimately lead him to the highest echelons of the legal profession.

Following his graduation from Harvard Law School in 1964, Breyer served as a law clerk for Supreme Court Justice Arthur Goldberg during the 1964-1965 term. This clerkship provided him with invaluable insight into the workings of the judicial system and exposed him to a wide range of legal issues at the highest level.

After his clerkship, Breyer transitioned to private practice, joining the law firm of Covington & Burling in Washington, D.C. As an associate at the firm, he worked on a variety of cases spanning corporate law, antitrust law, and administrative law.

His experience in private practice honed his legal skills and provided him with practical experience in navigating complex legal issues. In 1967, Breyer embarked on a new chapter in his career when he was appointed Assistant Special Prosecutor on the Watergate Special Prosecution Force.

In this role, he played a key role in investigating the Watergate scandal and prosecuting individuals implicated in the wrongdoing. Breyer's work on the Watergate investigation further solidified his reputation as a skilled and principled attorney committed to upholding the rule of law.

Following his tenure as Assistant Special Prosecutor, Breyer transitioned to academia, joining the faculty at Harvard Law School in 1967. As a professor, he taught courses on administrative law, regulatory policy, and antitrust law, among others.

Breyer's time at Harvard Law School allowed him to share his expertise with the next generation of legal scholars and practitioners while continuing to pursue his scholarly research interests.

In addition to his academic pursuits, Breyer also served in various government roles during this period. He held positions in the Department of Justice, including Assistant Special Prosecutor for the Watergate Special Prosecution Force and Chief Counsel to the Senate Judiciary Committee.

In these roles, Breyer played a key role in shaping legislation and policy on issues such as antitrust law, criminal justice reform, and judicial nominations.

Overall, Stephen Breyer's early career was marked by a diverse range of experiences that shaped his understanding of the law and prepared him for future leadership roles. From his clerkship at the Supreme Court to his work on the Watergate investigation and his tenure in academia and government service, Breyer's early career laid the groundwork for his later success as a jurist and public servant.

Chapter Three; Judicial Appointment

Stephen Breyer's ascent to the judiciary was a pivotal moment in his career, marked by a combination of professional accomplishment, political maneuvering, and public service. His journey from legal scholar to federal judge exemplifies the complex and often opaque process of judicial selection in the United States.

In 1980, Breyer's name was put forward as a nominee for the U.S. Court of Appeals for the First Circuit by President Jimmy Carter. This nomination was the culmination of years of dedication to the legal profession and a testament to Breyer's reputation as a respected legal scholar and practitioner.

Breyer's nomination to the federal bench was met with widespread acclaim from colleagues, legal scholars, and members of the legal community. His extensive experience in academia, government service, and private practice positioned him as a highly qualified candidate for the appellate court.

Throughout his confirmation process, Breyer faced scrutiny from senators and interest groups seeking to assess his judicial philosophy, temperament, and suitability for the federal judiciary. His hearings before the Senate Judiciary Committee provided an opportunity for senators to question him on a range of legal issues and to gauge his fitness for the bench.

Breyer's confirmation hearings were marked by a rigorous examination of his judicial record, legal writings, and personal beliefs. Senators sought to probe his views on constitutional interpretation, the role of the judiciary, and the application of legal precedent in shaping judicial decisions.

Despite some opposition from conservative senators, Breyer's nomination ultimately received bipartisan support, and he was confirmed by the Senate to the First Circuit Court of Appeals. His confirmation reflected a consensus among senators that Breyer possessed the qualifications, temperament, and integrity necessary to serve as a federal judge.

Breyer's tenure on the First Circuit Court of Appeals was characterized by a commitment to fairness, impartiality, and the rule of law. He approached each case with an open mind and a dedication to upholding the principles of justice and equality under the law.

As a federal appellate judge, Breyer authored numerous opinions on a wide range of legal issues, including civil rights, criminal law, administrative law, and constitutional law. His opinions reflected a thoughtful and pragmatic approach to legal interpretation, grounded in a deep understanding of legal precedent and a respect for the separation of powers.

Throughout his tenure on the First Circuit, Breyer earned a reputation as a fair and impartial jurist, respected by colleagues and litigants alike for his intellect, integrity, and judicial temperament.

His opinions were cited by legal scholars and practitioners as exemplars of clear and reasoned judicial analysis, contributing to the development of federal law in the areas within his jurisdiction. Breyer's service on the First Circuit Court of Appeals prepared him for the next phase of his judicial career: nomination to the Supreme Court of the United States.

In 1994, President Bill Clinton nominated Breyer to fill the vacancy left by retiring Associate Justice Harry Blackmun. Breyer's nomination to the Supreme Court was met with widespread praise from legal experts, politicians, and members of the public.

His extensive experience as a federal judge, combined with his scholarly achievements and commitment to public service, positioned him as a highly qualified candidate for the highest court in the land. During his confirmation hearings before the Senate Judiciary Committee, Breyer faced questions on a wide range of legal issues, including his views on constitutional interpretation, judicial activism, and the role of precedent in shaping judicial decisions.

Senators sought to assess Breyer's fitness for the Supreme Court and to ensure that he would uphold the principles of justice, fairness, and equality under the law. Despite some opposition from conservative senators, Breyer's nomination was ultimately confirmed by the Senate, and he was sworn in as an Associate Justice of the Supreme Court on August 3, 1994.

His confirmation marked the beginning of a distinguished tenure on the nation's highest court, where he would serve with distinction for nearly three decades. Moreover, Stephen Breyer's judicial appointment was a transformative moment in his career, catapulting him to the pinnacle of the legal profession and providing him with a platform to shape the course of American law for generations to come.

His confirmation to the federal bench reflected a consensus among senators that he possessed the intellect, integrity, and judicial temperament necessary to serve with distinction as a federal judge.

Throughout his tenure on the First Circuit Court of Appeals and later on the Supreme Court, Breyer remained committed to upholding the rule of law and the principles of justice, fairness, and equality under the law, leaving an indelible mark on the legal landscape of the United States.

Chapter Four; Supreme Court Tenure

Stephen Breyer's tenure on the Supreme Court of the United States spanned nearly three decades and was marked by a commitment to upholding the rule of law, fostering collegiality among his fellow justices, and grappling with some of the most pressing legal issues of our time.

As an Associate Justice of the Supreme Court, Breyer played a pivotal role in shaping the course of American jurisprudence and interpreting the Constitution in a manner consistent with its underlying principles.

Throughout his tenure on the Supreme Court, Breyer emerged as a pragmatic and thoughtful voice on the bench, known for his meticulous approach to legal reasoning and his willingness to engage with complex legal issues.

He approached each case with an open mind and a dedication to applying the law fairly and impartially, regardless of the political implications or public opinion. Breyer's opinions on the Supreme Court reflected his commitment to judicial restraint and respect for precedent, as well as his belief in the importance of considering the practical consequences of legal decisions.

He often emphasized the need for the Court to take into account the real-world impact of its rulings on individuals, communities, and society as a whole. One of the hallmarks of Breyer's jurisprudence was his advocacy for a pragmatic and context-sensitive approach to constitutional interpretation.

He believed that the Constitution should be interpreted in light of evolving societal norms, technological advancements, and changing circumstances, rather than rigidly adhering to originalist or textualist interpretations. Throughout his tenure, Breyer authored numerous majority opinions, concurrences, and dissents on a wide range of legal issues, including civil rights, environmental law, administrative law, and criminal justice.

His opinions were characterized by clear and reasoned analysis, grounded in a deep understanding of legal precedent and a respect for the separation of powers.

One of the key themes of Breyer's jurisprudence was his commitment to protecting individual rights and liberties, particularly in cases involving civil liberties, privacy rights, and equal protection under the law. He was a staunch advocate for the rights of marginalized and vulnerable populations, often siding with the liberal wing of the Court in cases involving issues such as affirmative action, LGBTQ rights, and reproductive rights.

Breyer also played a pivotal role in shaping the Court's approach to statutory interpretation, advocating for a pragmatic and functional approach that prioritized legislative intent and the broader purposes of the law.

He believed that statutes should be interpreted in a manner that best advances the underlying goals of the legislative body that enacted them, rather than strictly adhering to textualist or formalist interpretations. In addition to his judicial responsibilities, Breyer also played an active role in fostering collegiality and consensus among his fellow justices.

He was known for his collaborative approach to decision-making, often seeking common ground with his colleagues and working to bridge ideological divides on the Court.

Breyer's tenure on the Supreme Court was not without controversy, however, as he occasionally found himself in the minority in closely divided cases with significant legal and social implications. Despite this, he remained steadfast in his commitment to the principles of justice, fairness, and equality under the law, often using his dissents as a platform to articulate his views and defend the rights of the disadvantaged.

Throughout his tenure, Breyer's influence extended beyond the confines of the courtroom, as he sought to engage with the public and educate citizens about the role of the judiciary in American society.

He frequently delivered lectures, wrote articles, and participated in public forums, sharing his insights on legal issues and promoting public understanding of the law.

In addition, Stephen Breyer's tenure on the Supreme Court was defined by his commitment to upholding the rule of law, fostering consensus among his colleagues, and advocating for a pragmatic and context-sensitive approach to constitutional interpretation.

His legacy as an Associate Justice will endure for generations to come, as his opinions and jurisprudence continue to shape the course of American law and society.

Chapter Five; Legacy and Impact

Stephen Breyer's legacy as a jurist and public servant is multifaceted, reflecting his profound impact on American law, jurisprudence, and the broader legal landscape.

Throughout his distinguished career, Breyer left an indelible mark on the judiciary and society as a whole, shaping the course of American jurisprudence and advancing the cause of justice and equality under the law. One of Breyer's most enduring contributions to the legal profession was his commitment to upholding the rule of law and protecting individual rights and liberties.

As an Associate Justice of the Supreme Court, Breyer authored numerous opinions that expanded and protected fundamental rights, including freedom of speech, privacy rights, and equal protection under the law.

His opinions were characterized by a deep respect for precedent and a commitment to applying the law fairly and impartially, regardless of the political implications or public opinion. Breyer's legacy also extends to his advocacy for a pragmatic and context-sensitive approach to constitutional interpretation.

He believed that the Constitution should be interpreted in light of evolving societal norms, technological advancements, and changing circumstances, rather than rigidly adhering to originalist or textualist interpretations.

This approach to constitutional interpretation has had a profound impact on the Court's jurisprudence and has shaped the way in which legal scholars and practitioners approach the Constitution In addition to his contributions to constitutional law, Breyer's legacy is also evident in his work on statutory interpretation and administrative law.

He advocated for a functional and pragmatic approach to interpreting statutes, emphasizing the importance of legislative intent and the broader purposes of the law. His opinions in cases involving administrative law have provided important guidance on the scope of executive power and the role of administrative agencies in implementing and enforcing federal law.

Breyer's impact on American law and society is perhaps most evident in his advocacy for a more just and equitable legal system. Throughout his career, he has been a vocal proponent of equal justice under the law, advocating for reforms to address systemic inequalities and disparities in the criminal justice system.

He has spoken out against racial discrimination, excessive sentencing, and the death penalty, arguing that these practices undermine the principles of fairness and due process.

Breyer's commitment to justice and equality under the law is also reflected in his efforts to promote access to justice and expand legal representation for underserved communities. He has been a strong advocate for legal aid programs, pro bono services, and initiatives aimed at improving access to legal services for low-income individuals and marginalized communities.

His advocacy has helped to ensure that all Americans have access to the legal resources and representation they need to protect their rights and interests. Beyond his contributions to the law, Breyer's legacy is also evident in his efforts to foster collegiality and consensus among his fellow justices on the Supreme Court.

He was known for his collaborative approach to decision-making, often seeking common ground with his colleagues and working to bridge ideological divides on the Court. His efforts to promote civility and cooperation among the justices have helped to maintain the integrity and effectiveness of the Court as an institution.

In addition to his impact on the judiciary, Breyer's legacy is also evident in his role as a public intellectual and educator. Throughout his career, he has been a vocal advocate for public understanding of the law, frequently delivering lectures, writing articles, and participating in public forums to educate citizens about the role of the judiciary in American society.

His efforts to promote legal literacy and civic engagement have helped to empower citizens to participate in the democratic process and advocate for justice and equality under the law. Furthermore, Stephen Breyer's legacy as a jurist and public servant is profound and far-reaching, reflecting his enduring commitment to justice, equality, and the rule of law.

Through his jurisprudence, advocacy, and public engagement, Breyer has left an indelible mark on American law and society, shaping the course of jurisprudence and advancing the cause of justice and equality for future generations.

Chapter Six; Personal Life

Stephen Breyer's personal life is a testament to the values of family, friendship, and lifelong learning that have guided him throughout his career as a jurist and public servant. Despite the demands of his professional responsibilities, Breyer has always made time for his loved ones and pursued his passions outside of the courtroom.

Born on August 15, 1938, in San Francisco, California, Breyer was raised in a close-knit family environment. His parents instilled in him a strong work ethic, a sense of integrity, and a deep appreciation for education and intellectual curiosity. Breyer fondly recalls spending time with his parents and siblings, cherishing the moments spent exploring the city and engaging in family activities.

Throughout his life, Breyer has maintained strong ties to his family, finding solace and support in their love and companionship. He credits his family with providing him with the foundation and encouragement to pursue his dreams and aspirations, both personally and professionally.

In addition to his family, Breyer has also cultivated meaningful relationships with friends, colleagues, and mentors throughout his life. He values the importance of camaraderie and collaboration, recognizing the vital role that interpersonal connections play in fostering personal growth and fulfillment.

Breyer's friendships extend beyond the confines of the courtroom, as he has forged lasting bonds with individuals from diverse backgrounds and walks of life. He cherishes the opportunity to engage with others, sharing stories, experiences, and insights that enrich his understanding of the world and deepen his appreciation for human connection.

Outside of his professional duties, Breyer is an avid reader and lifelong learner, with a voracious appetite for knowledge and discovery. He enjoys exploring a wide range of subjects, from history and philosophy to literature and the arts, finding inspiration and enlightenment in the written word.

Breyer's passion for learning extends to his personal interests and hobbies, which include music, travel, and the outdoors. He finds joy and rejuvenation in experiencing new cultures, landscapes, and experiences, embracing the opportunity to broaden his horizons and expand his worldview.

Despite the demands of his busy schedule, Breyer makes time for leisure and relaxation, recognizing the importance of balance and self-care in maintaining his health and well-being. He enjoys spending time with his family and friends, savoring moments of quiet reflection and connection amidst the hustle and bustle of daily life.

Breyer's personal life is also enriched by his love of the arts, particularly music and literature. He finds solace and inspiration in the beauty and creativity of artistic expression, drawing strength and sustenance from the power of human imagination and emotion.

In his free time, Breyer can often be found attending concerts, visiting museums, or immersing himself in a good book. He values the transformative power of art and literature to transcend boundaries, spark dialogue, and foster empathy and understanding among people of diverse backgrounds and perspectives.

Moreso, Stephen Breyer's personal life is a reflection of his values, passions, and priorities outside of the courtroom. He treasures his relationships with family and friends, cherishes the opportunity to engage with others, and finds fulfillment and joy in lifelong learning, exploration, and the pursuit of artistic expression. Through his personal pursuits and interests, Breyer exemplifies the importance of balance, connection, and enrichment in leading a meaningful and fulfilling life.

Chapter Seven; Retirement and Post-Court Activities

Stephen Breyer's retirement from the Supreme Court marked the end of a distinguished judicial career that spanned nearly three decades. While his departure from the bench signaled the closing of one chapter in his life, it also heralded the beginning of a new phase filled with opportunities for continued engagement, service, and exploration.

Following his retirement, Breyer wasted no time in embarking on a variety of post-court activities aimed at continuing his lifelong commitment to public service, legal scholarship, and civic engagement. Despite stepping down from the bench, Breyer remained as active and engaged as ever, leveraging his expertise and experience to make a positive impact on the world beyond the confines of the courtroom.

One of the primary ways in which Breyer has remained engaged in public life post-retirement is through his writing and public speaking engagements. Drawing on his extensive experience as a jurist and legal scholar, Breyer has authored several books and articles on a wide range of legal topics, including constitutional law, statutory interpretation, and the role of the judiciary in American society.

In addition to his scholarly pursuits, Breyer has also been an active participant in public forums, lectures, and panel discussions, where he shares his insights and perspectives on pressing legal and social issues. His public speaking engagements have provided him with a platform to engage with audiences from diverse backgrounds and to promote public understanding of the law and the role of the judiciary in American democracy.

Breyer's retirement has also afforded him the opportunity to pursue his passions and interests outside of the legal profession. An avid reader and lifelong learner, Breyer has continued to indulge his love of literature, music, and the arts, finding inspiration and enrichment in cultural experiences and artistic expression.

In addition to his personal interests, Breyer has also remained active in various philanthropic and charitable endeavors, supporting causes and organizations that align with his values and priorities. He has been a vocal advocate for access to justice, legal aid, and civic education, working to promote equal justice under the law and to empower individuals and communities to exercise their rights and freedoms.

Despite his retirement from the bench, Breyer has continued to play a role in shaping the future of the legal profession and the judiciary. He has served as a mentor and advisor to aspiring lawyers and law students, sharing his wisdom and experience with the next generation of legal scholars and practitioners.

Breyer's retirement has also provided him with the opportunity to spend more time with his family and loved ones, cherishing moments of togetherness and connection that were often overshadowed by the demands of his professional responsibilities. He values the opportunity to savor life's simple pleasures and to create lasting memories with those he holds dear.

In essence, Stephen Breyer's retirement from the Supreme Court has not marked the end of his contributions to society, but rather the beginning of a new chapter filled with opportunities for continued engagement, service, and exploration.

Through his writing, speaking engagements, philanthropic endeavors, and personal pursuits, Breyer remains as active and committed as ever to making a positive impact on the world and shaping the future of the legal profession and the judiciary.

Conclusion

In concluding this biography of Stephen Breyer, it is evident that his life and career have been marked by a profound commitment to justice, integrity, and public service. From his humble beginnings in San Francisco to his tenure on the Supreme Court of the United States, Breyer has embodied the values of fairness, compassion, and intellectual curiosity that define the best of the legal profession.

Throughout his life, Breyer has been guided by a strong sense of purpose and a belief in the power of the law to effect positive change in society. From his early days as a law clerk to his service on the federal bench, Breyer has approached each challenge with dedication, diligence, and a commitment to upholding the principles of justice and equality under the law.

As an Associate Justice of the Supreme Court, Breyer played a pivotal role in shaping the course of American jurisprudence, advocating for a pragmatic and context-sensitive approach to constitutional interpretation.

His opinions on the Court reflected a deep respect for precedent, a commitment to fairness, and a recognition of the practical consequences of legal decisions on individuals and communities. Beyond his judicial responsibilities, Breyer has been a tireless advocate for access to justice, legal aid, and civic education, working to ensure that all Americans have the opportunity to exercise their rights and freedoms.

He has been a vocal proponent of equal justice under the law, speaking out against systemic inequalities and disparities in the criminal justice system. In addition to his contributions to the law, Breyer's personal life is a testament to the importance of family, friendship, and lifelong learning.

He values the opportunity to spend time with loved ones, indulge his passions, and engage with the world around him. Despite the demands of his professional responsibilities, Breyer has remained grounded and connected to the people and experiences that bring him joy and fulfillment.

As readers, you have embarked on a journey through the life and career of one of the most influential jurists of our time. Along the way, you have gained insights into Breyer's character, values, and contributions to the legal profession and society as a whole.

Your engagement with this odyssey is a testament to your own curiosity, intellect, and commitment to learning. On behalf of the author, I would like to express my heartfelt gratitude to you, the readers, for joining us on this odyssey. Your interest and engagement have been a source of inspiration and encouragement throughout the writing process.

I hope that this biography has provided you with a deeper understanding of Stephen Breyer's life and legacy, as well as insights into the principles and ideals that have guided him along the way. As we reach the conclusion of this book, I invite you to reflect on the lessons and insights you have gained from Breyer's life and career.

May his dedication to justice, integrity, and public service continue to inspire us all to strive for a more just, equitable, and compassionate society. Thank you once again for accompanying us on this journey. May you carry the spirit of Stephen Breyer's legacy with you as you continue your own odyssey through life.

www.ingramcontent.com/pod-product-compliance
Lightning Source LLC
Chambersburg PA
CBHW070413230526
45471CB00006B/2782